Universa

Chakra Energy Activating,
Cleansing & Healing Affirmations...

Author & Illustrator: Michelle -J-Summers

©Universal You 2017

Content

From the Author
Acknowledgements
How to use this book

Introduction..8

Root Chakra Cleansing, Healing & Activating Affirmations 21

Sacral Chakra Cleansing, Healing & Activating Affirmations 34

Solar Plexus Cleansing, Healing & Activating Affirmations 47

Heart Chakra Cleansing, Healing & Activating Affirmations 58

Throat Chakra Cleansing, Healing & Activating Affirmations 69

Third Eye Chakra Cleansing, Healing & Activating Affirmations 80

Crown Chakra Cleansing, Healing & Activating Affirmations 93

Spiritual Strenghthening & Healing Affirmations 104

Virtue Bank of Positive Words 114

Additional Universal You Books 127

From the Author

When the student is ready to learn it's a well-known fact that the teacher will appear. The fact that you're now reading this book means you're ready to take the next steps in your personal evolutionary journey.

Chakra cleansing and activating affirmations book was created to bring you a sense of inner alignment, balance, bliss, harmony, security, peace, and bring about a deeper connection to your mind, body and spirit. Daily practice and use of affirmations will assist you to turn around your attitude, as well as your world in no time. These affirmations are designed to support and assist you in clearing blockages of negative energies, as well as assist you with resetting negative thought patterns, and turning them into positive new patterns. Finally, affirmations will aid you in raising your awareness and natural vibration higher so to reach optimal energy levels within, and connect with the collective consciousness of unconditional love and oneness..

Acknowledgements

Beloved readers may the seeds of Sources, love, truth and wisdoms be planted within your hearts & minds, so that they can take deepest roots within your being, in-order to blossom into your reality.

May all Sources seeds walk in the love, light, glory & grace of God on Gaia. May you all give and receive love unconditionally in abundance, with compassion & kindness. May you all gift blessing of forgiveness unto each other, and in return may you be blessed with love and light unconditionally from the Supreme oneness of the universal Source from the highest heaven.

I would like to express my greatest gratitude to all soul's that have collectively supported me along my journey. From my family, soul friends, and all other souls we have encountered, at the many crossroads on each of our evolutionary journeys throughout life.

I would also like to acknowledge and thank "God our entire Universe", as I am truly grateful for all lessons I have been taught in life, and while building this book especially. I am thankful I am able to be in light and love, so to turn these lessons in my life into blessings that I have shared collectively, and are able to teach others with, in return as I grow into, and as ONE.

You are all "Energy magnetic manifesting Magicians". Collectively we are free.. So, I give great thanks to all the free thinkers of this World who seek "The Truth", and to all the beautiful souls reading this book, and making a difference in the world right now. Infinite Love & Light – Universal You: M-J-Summers..

How to use this book

The teachings found within this book can be explored and used by the reader, in whichever way resonates with the individual soul.

One may choose to open this book and read from the beginning to the end in a regulated fashion. Or you may choose to become creative and use this book as an Oracle guide, by requesting to the Universe or Higher Self before opening its pages, which affirmation pages will serve soul best in one's present? Ask for this inner guidance before opening the book randomly to a page guided in response to your question. You are invited to become as creative as you can be with this book.

This most important piece of information to remember is, to be fully in one's faith, mindful, and always in one's truth, with an open heart, and mind in one's present. Remaining positive while fullest faith is placed and trusted in the process of the "Universe", "Source" and "Self" to deliver.

Introduction

If you believe the phrase "you are what you think", then life truly stems from your thoughts. We cannot purely rely on thoughts; we must translate thoughts into feelings, words, and eventually into actions to manifest our intentions. This means we must be very careful with our words, choosing to speak only to those of higher vibration, words which work towards the benefit of our personal evolution, and ultimately cultivate our experiences for the highest good for all.

Our own negative thought patterns affect the health of our body, mind, and spirit. Basically, you're creating uneasiness, or "disease" in your body by the way you think, feel, and approach each situation in your life.

Affirmations help purify our thought patterns, and restructure the dynamic of our mind, emotions and behaviours, so that we truly begin to think nothing is impossible. The word affirmation comes from the Latin affirmare, originally meaning "to make steady, to strengthen."

Contrary to popular belief, affirmations and the power of positive thought is not a new age technique. It can in fact be traced back hundreds of years to the ancient east in which it is believed they are closely related to "Mantras" (Mantras are symbols, patterns, or poems repeated during meditation). "Mantras" being Sanskrit for "Man" to think "Tra" to liberate, meaning it is an avenue to free one's mind from thoughts. Affirmations, and the power of positive thought, also

have some serious scientific backing in the form of Neuroscience (The scientific study of the bodies nervous system).

In the 1970's, in the University of Santa Cruz, two scientists by the names of John Grinder and Richard Bandler, the creators of "NLP"- Neuro-Linguistic-Programming, an approach to communication, personal development and psychotherapy.) After studying the most exceptional and successful psychotherapists they theorized that success can be achieved by increasing positive behaviours, and decreasing negative ones. These scientists found that there is a connection between neurological processes (Neuro-), language (linguistic), behavioural patterns learned through experience (programming), and that these can be changed to achieve specific goals in life. NLP methodology can model the skills of exceptional people, allowing anyone to acquire those skills.

The power of affirmations has been well documented for decades now, but a critical part of their effectiveness is to ensure that the affirmation is custom designed for the individual. With that being said the affirmations ring true, and natural when repeated habitually.

We must believe to receive, so we don't undermine the value of affirmation rituals by expecting them to provide quick fixes, but more so to establish a clear mental pathway between what we need, want, and what we believe we are worthy of. An affirmation should never be, "I want more Money", it should be "I am worthy of more success". Or "I am happy and grateful for all that I have"

In the history of affirmations, the word "Abracadabra" is a word of "double power". It unites the microcosm (Inner Cosmos) with the macrocosm (Outer Cosmos). This is represented by the pentagram and the hexagram, the rose, and the cross, the circle and the Square. The 5 and the 6, also called the attainment of knowledge, and the conversation of one's "Holy Guardian Angel". – The word is a symbol of the establishment of the pillar, or phallus of the macrocosm in the void of the microcosm. Here are a few examples.

- It's from the phrase "Avrakehdabra" meaning "I will create as I speak".

- The source is three Hebrew words "ab" (Father) "ben" (Son) and "Ruachacadosh" (Holy Spirit)
- It's from Chaldean "Abbada Kedabra", meaning "Perish like the word".
- It originated with a Gnostic sect in Alexandria called the "Basilidians" and was based on "Abrasax" the name of their Supreme Deity ("Abraxas in Latin sources).

Creating Affirmations

The practice of affirmations will bring a positive change in your lives for the better. When we are truly ready and willing to do what it takes to create change for the better of all, we are ready to set the affirmation process into motion. To do this, we use a combination of the laws within our universe. One in particular called the "law of attraction." I am sure most are aware of this law.

Basically, this law states that we attract into our lives whatever we focus our attention and energy on.

To create an affirmation correctly, the first part of your affirmation should connect your physical mind in present (conscious – mind) to your divine self (subconscious – mind), or in enlightened cases (super-subconscious –mind).

For example: To bring one's divinity into present, by becoming thankful for what you are about to receive. So, here is an example as to how, I would start my affirmation.: "Thank you", "Thank you", and "Thank you". "I am one with the Divine Creator of the Universe; I am "Grateful" for all souls made of pure love and light".

The second part of your affirmation should correct the negative thought pattern you are trying to change. This is usually done on a subtle level, as you don't want to put extra focus on the negative pattern, but rather to new, correct positive patterns you want to replace old ones with. If you're trying to stop being a resentful person let's say, you wouldn't focus on the negative aspects, but rather your affirmation should focus on the new positive aspects, and experiences you want to have.

Another example of this would be "I create a life filled with love and joy. I am happy for every good, or great achievement I've achieved, and that's achieved daily by all good souls."

You want to turn these new thought patterns into energy then you must, feel them by trying to visualise these achievements gained. You must try and remember how you felt when you did achieve something great, or try to create the feeling of how you will feel when you do achieve your goals. You can also bring the feelings to light, when you recall memories of a time when a loved one achieved something great. The key is you must project the feelings to match the frequency of the thoughts, to whatever it is you want to match or manifest into your existence.

The third part of a successful affirmation is to combine thoughts and feelings into action.

Another example on how to do this: Is to use the magic of spelling, one would write their intention repeatedly, while feeding the intention energy, in-order to cast a desire or a spell into the universe. It will give the affirmation more energy and momentum the more you feel, think, and write it into existence as if it already existed. Then as if by magic, it soon will.

The fourth and final part of your affirmation is to set the affirmation in motion. We must speak the intention into existence, as we act and work daily towards achieving our goals we have set in this affirmation.

The more you speak of it as already being so, the universe has no other option but to deliver what your subconscious is telling God you need.

As God listens, as does our living universe, and what you must believe it will be delivered.

The universe is always reacting to what you say, feel, think, and do.

The best way to finish your affirmation is with "so it is".

"As above so below". Your finished affirmation would look something like this...

"Thank you, Thank you, and Thank you"
" I am one with the Divine Creator of the universe; I am grateful for all souls made of pure love and Light."
I create a life filled with love and joy,
I am happy for every good achievement achieved by all good souls
I am happy and see beauty in all things,
so be it
as above so below".

A reminder; A good affirmation technique requires genuine conviction, energy, focus, and a mindful attitude to maximise the potency of the words you speak. It is important not to trivialise, or undermine the intention behind the words. It is vital to this practice that the language is true to the subconscious, as well as the conscious mind.

Visualisation

Visualisation is key to many spiritual practices, and is essential in spiritual development. We should always recognize truth for what it is, whether we like it or not. If a situation is bad, we should not pretend that it isn't. But – we can, through positive visualization, make a positive impact on that bad situation.

In prayer we should always visualize the people or situations we are trying to heal or uplift, as being filled with golden or white light, and as being better than they currently are. Thoughts are energy; every time we think a thought it influences our environment, be it better or worse. Positive thoughts, have a positive effect on everything and everyone around us. There are many successful people of this age who deem their abundant careers to the powers of visualisation.

Below I have added two inspirational examples.

This will give you a greater understanding of how you are an individual creator in a quantum universe. Once you master your personal energy and combine them with all universal laws.

Jim Carrey

Jim Carrey used the power of visualization to keep himself focused on his goals by writing down the exact amount of money he wanted to make on a cheque which was entitled, "acting services rendered" and amazingly, ended up achieving the exact amount he wrote down 10 years later. He would also drive to a location in the Hollywood hills and visualise the lifestyle he would've liked. Jim even stated that his return home was wonderful, because he felt like all the wonderful things, he had visualized were now a reality. He would literally not let himself go home, until he truly believed his mind. When you visualize your dreams, you begin to align yourself with the universe to make them a reality.

"It is better to risk starving to death then surrender. If you give up on your dreams, what's left?"

~ Jim Carrey ~

Albert Einstein

One of the little-known facts about Albert Einstein is that he attended a school that followed the teaching methods of the Swiss educator Johann Pestalozzi. Pestalozzi schools' taught children in what was known as the Pestalozzi method (the "Method"). Under the Method, it was believed that instead of dealing with words, children should learn through activity and objects. They should be free to pursue their own interests, and reach their own conclusions.

Much of Pestalozzi's teaching methods can be found in a book he published in 1801, called "How Gertrude Teaches Her Children". In this book, he discusses the importance of spontaneity and additionally allowing children to investigate the subject, and arrive at any conclusions, or outcomes themselves. Visualization was a major component in this method. Pestalozzi believed that visualization was among the mind's most powerful features, and that imagery was where all knowledge started.

"Imagination is everything. It is the preview of life's coming attractions".   -Albert Einstein -

Practice with affirmations daily will support the reader to build a solid foundation & bridge, that can connect one deeper to their inner essence and the oneness within all things within the Universe.

Affirmations are a fantastic starting point for anyone's spiritual practices to take root and blossom on Gaia. Affirmations mixed with a positive attitude is a spiritual recipe made to feed the inner seed and assist one's inner abilities within the sacred process to spiritually transform

There is no separation. All is one, and the one is all. All life is Gods dream, and you are a collective character and creator within it.

Have fun with it!

Love & Light

MJ oxox

Root Chakra Healing & Activating Affirmations

Affirmations used daily for the Root Chakra will help you to open, cleanse, clear, and generate new energies that will ultimately bring positive experiences for you. You will start to feel spiritually supported from within, you will regain a deeper sense of security and trust, that already resides within you!!

- As I start my spiritual journey, raising my vibration as well as awareness, I become stronger in myself, and my surroundings support me fully.
- Today I will make a mental list of 5 things I am truly grateful for, and I will do this daily from now on.
- I am grateful for my shelter, and the sleep space it provides me.
- I am aligning and activating my Root chakra, it is now opening.
- I feel secure, and I am always supported and loved.
- I am safe, and at peace in my space always.
- I am nurtured by nature; its fruits nourish my body, blood and bones.
- I am grounded and firmly rooted to mother Gaia's energies.
- I am not afraid to project my personal power.
- I am strong. I am stable. I am secure, I am love, and I am safe.
- I am connected fully to the universe as I am my very own energetic, magnetic compass. I attract all good.
- I am grounded and I am centred.
- I am safe and supported by the universe.

- I am exactly where I need to be in this present moment.
- I am connected to the earth, and I feel safe.
- I am at peace with my surroundings.
- I am revitalised and energised, each day Gaia rejuvenates my energy.
- I am connected and fully aware of my mind and the feelings I generate. I am deeply rooted into earth.
- I am safe in my body, I am letting go of any fears.
- I am financially secure because I have what I need in the present.
- I am protected and nurtured by the universe.
- I am grounded and I am strong deeply rooted into Gaia. I am thankful for all nature provides.
- I am grounded, centred, and connected to the earth.
- The earth supports, nourishes, and nurtures me. I grow strong from all the natural energies I can thankfully source.
- I stand authentically in my person, and understand my power; I belong here in this present.
- I love who I am. I am never alone.
- My mind, body, and soul are safe and supported.

- My body is strong and healthy.
- My body is a temple, and I worship my highest astral self. As above, I am so below.
- I have an abundance of strength. I have confidence, and I have more than enough.
- I have prosperity, and I have a strong foundation to work from.
- I have strength and courage. I have a right to be here as much as the next being.
- I can trust myself to make the best choice as I become grounded.
- All is well, I am well. My space is free and a safe place to be.
- I am becoming fearless. I can be courageous and compassionate at the same time.
- I live life to the fullest. I live a good life. I am grateful to be alive.
- I have security and protection. I have more than enough prosperity and abundance.
- I have confidence and motivation.
- I call forth, the purest love and light, to guide me on my journey home.
- I stand my ground. I feel safe in nature.

- I am present. I am firmly rooted in Gaia's energies.
- I am nurtured. I am at one with nature and nature is at one with me.
- I feel deeply connected, as my spirit is grounded into the core of mother earth. I am rooted firmly.
- I am free to be above as below, connected to the God and Goddess
- I love being in my body. I respect my body.
- I understand my bodies needs perfectly. If I silence my mind and listen to it, I can do what's best for me.
- I have shelter. I am very grateful for this gift.
- I am secure where I am in this present moment.
- I have no fear in this present moment
- I am liberated in this present moment from fear.
- I love, respect, and accept myself for who I am today and every day.
- I do not need anyone's approval to be me.
- I manifest things through my thoughts, feelings, and actions.
- I am letting go of any stress, as it no longer serves me. I choose not to fear today.
- I am open to new ideas. I am open to new experiences.

- I am now opening my root chakra energy centre. I am becoming more mindful of my present thoughts and feelings.
- I am no longer worried about tomorrow, because I live for today. I understand my happiness today, is my experience tomorrow.
- I do not attach to material items in this world. I know what is really important.
- I am becoming more adventurous and fearless.
- I know it is safe to take risks. If my intuition tells me I am able to do so.
- I am gaining a different perspective on nature.
- I am now feeling at one with the cycles and seasons.
- I am starting to see things through a caring nature.
- I am learning to let go of judgement.
- I am as strong as a tree rooted in Gaia. I respect all living creatures.
- I am a loving and supporting person, of myself and my family.
- I am hopeful for my future.
- I am speaking less, and listening more.
- I am now living in harmony and natural flow with all movement.

- I release any tension, as this no longer serves me.
- I have an enhanced sense of smell.
- I am exactly where I need to be at this present time.
- I have all the support I could need, at any given time.
- I am passionate and true with who I am.
- I am always protected by the purest love and light.
- I am starting to see life in a brighter way.
- I am an expression of creation, and creation is an expression through me.
- I am attending this school called life. I learn from the present lessons daily. I look at all things, and find the positive polarity.
- In this reality, I am safe and secure.
- I now live my life based on trust, and not in fear of something or someone else.
- I lost fear and gained trust.
- I spend more time doing things to benefit me and my journey.
- I realise what is not important for my wellbeing on this journey.
- I honour the feminine and masculine within me. I am of love, not lust.

- I am recognising my gifts are of many. I am slowly transforming.
- I am strong, radiant, and a beautiful soul.
- I am able to rest comfortably on Gaia when I need to.
- I am starting to sleep so much better each night.
- I am able to intuitively know where my journey starts in each new morning. I visualise the positive experiences the night before.
- I am a sensual being. I can express myself with style and grace.
- I am organised and ready for each new day.
- I do my very best in each new day.
- I know what I need. I attract what needs me also in return. All my needs are fulfilled.
- I am responsible for my own life. I am happy to help others that need me.
- I am letting go of anger, as this no longer serves me.
- I need only positive things that will enhance my experience here on earth, and others experiences combined with mine.

- I am letting go of all negative things, people, places, and memories, over all space times that no longer serve me.
- I am sharing and caring towards my brothers and sisters of earth.
- I am now open to new ideas and experiences.
- I am comfortable in life. I am trying my very best in each present moment.
- I am open to meeting new people.
- I am becoming calmer in each new day. I am now more understanding and able to control my negative thought patterns. I am in control of how I want to think, act and react to any present situation.
- I lost fear. I am gaining an abundance of confidence.
- I am now building a new, stronger foundation for my inner home here on Gaia.
- I am open to receiving all the experiences I am meant to have, here in the present moment.

- I am open to learning new things every day.
- I realise I am here to learn and grow, in doing so I can share with others my wisdom as I go.
- I am starting to feel at one again, finding inner ways to positively deal with life's experiences.
- I am beginning to master meditation.
- I am free to be whoever I want to be.
- I am wealthy with everything I have. I am grateful.
- I am grateful for all I have and have experienced in the past, and for everything I will experience in the future. I am so very happy to be alive.
- I am becoming who I was meant to be, I am aligning with my highest purpose and souls' mission.
- I belong in the world at this present time.
- I am letting go of any hate I have, or have carried, for this is not good for my health. This negative energy no longer serves me.
- I feel secure where I am at present.
- I am compassionate. I am kind to others.
- My spirit is grounded deep in Gaia. I am free to grow in her garden.
- I feel my connection to everything else on earth.

- I am open to change. I do not fear my survival.
- I realise that whatever my past worries were, they created any present obstacles. I can finally let go of worry.
- I am thankful for each new day in life, and the treasures buried in its deepest oceans.
- I let go of any blockages, and release these with love and gratitude
- I am no longer stagnant. I realise everything is in constant movement. I now go forward with this continual energy flow.
- I am the only master of my reality.
- I have self-control. I am balanced.
- I have energy and vitality. I have strength and courage.
- I have safety and stability. I am blessed.
- I let go of my past, and welcome my future.
- I am safe in my environment. I let go of any worries that no longer serve me.
- I am a spiritual being on earth, having a human experience. I am free to be. As we all are.

- I have grown stronger and stronger in each new day. I am grounded to Gaia, and energized by her golden energy daily.
- I have started the journey to heal my mind, body and soul. I am embarking on a wonderful spiritual journey.
- I am safe and secure in the knowledge of who I am at this present time.
- I am developing a sense of what I must do next on my path. As I move forwards happily as one with each step taken, I become a step closer to home on the journey.
- My senses are starting to awaken, and my root chakra is opened and activated. I am developing a greater sense of smell, as my senses start to heighten.

Daily practice of these particular affirmations will assist you to turn around your attitude, as well as your world in no time.... These affirmations are designed to support you with clearing negative energies and thought patterns, as well as aid you in raising your awareness and natural vibration higher, so to reach optimal energy levels within. This will ultimately have a positive effect on your experiences within your outer life. This chapter will ultimately have a positive effect on what you can attract and experience in life, when you are grounded and mindful.

Sacral Chakra Healing & Activating Affirmations

Affirmations for the Sacral Chakra will help you to open, cleanse, clear, and generate new energies in present, that will ultimately bring positive experiences for your future. You are continually creating daily as you think, speak, and act now. When this energy centre is balanced, this will create a more positive and emotionally stable you.

- I am continually moving forward with positive actions. I am aligning and activating my Sacral chakra.
- I am opening my sacral chakra, and balancing its energy. I feel completely connected, and I am one with the cycle of all.
- I am creating my future with my present actions, feelings, thought, and words. I am free from negative energies and emotions. Every day I live in my bliss, filled with natural energies and tranquillity.
- I am confident within my sexuality. I express myself freely.
- An abundance of energies flow to, and through me in great volumes.
- I feel loved and secure. My body is sacred.
- I feel blessed and happy. I am one with the divine feminine and masculine that is within me.
- I feel nourished and free, just to be me.
- I honour myself. I respect and enjoy my creative, emotional, and healing abilities.
- I am cleansing and clearing my sacral chakra each day.
- I am grounded in all I do, and free to just be me.

- I feel joyful and passionate. I feel safe and secure in this life.
- I feel safe in my body. I feel free to choose what's right for me.
- I am abundance in this life. My energy is the abundance source. I am grateful to know my worth.
- I feel comfortable in my own body.
- I feel nurtured and protected.
- I am opening and activating my sacral chakra.
- I feel pleasure in my body.
- I feel sensual within my being. I feel energetic. I feel empathy.
- I feel and express my creativity.
- I feel a natural sense of joy each day.
- My sexuality is sacred to me. I share only with soul mates, that I connect deeply too.
- My senses are awakened and becoming more active.
- My life is filled with joy. I know what I need.
- My intuition guides me successfully on my journey.
- I am cleansing and clearing my sacral chakra daily.
- My intuitive senses are awakened, and growing stronger.

- I enjoy all the sensations in and around my body.
- I love, honour, and respect myself.
- I sense my connection to my body and the earth.
- I release all, that does not serve my highest good.
- I feel a sense of beauty within, and all around me.
- I allow my intuition to guide me daily.
- I allow my emotions to flow through me in a positive way, letting go of negative ones, as I adopt new ways to react to my emotions, as I become more mindful.
- I feel healed and whole. I am full of optimism for my future. My sacral chakra is aligned and opened.
- I embrace my sexuality. I am opening my sacral chakra to love only, and passion as I leave lust in the past.
- I am grounded to Gaia, in every present second of each new day.
- I am cleansing and clearing my sacral energy centre, and working to raise my inner vibration higher.
- I am aligning to live the life I am intended to be living, here and now. I am in flow with my destiny.

- I am harmonizing with everything that brings great joy to me. I only attract the highest vibration souls into my experience.
- I am finding new things daily, that bring me greatest pleasures.
- I am starting to feel more connected to all things in nature. I feel more natural. I am now becoming one with all things.
- I am beginning to find my own way in the world.
- I am becoming a stronger version of my truest self. I am becoming more aware and woke to my inner intuition.
- I am taking back control over all the conscious choices that I make in my life for me.
- I have a new found burning passion for life, and to live it fully.
- I am full of vitality, and have a magical passion for all life. I project my gratitude out into the universe daily.
- I know exactly what I am doing and where I am going in my life.
- I live in my own bliss. I do not judge anyone.

- My mind is creative. I choose what's best for me daily to grow.
- I am an affectionate person. I choose to be so
- I have consideration for myself and others always.
- I am always considering others feelings. I encourage all to grow equally, towards living in peace as one.
- I am beginning to change the form of my being. I am thinking more positive thinking patterns.
- I am becoming aware of my inner building blocks and the universal elements that make me who I am. Earth, Air, Water, Fire and Spirit.
- I am becoming each new day emotionally stable and grounded.
- I am able to understand my emotions easier. I am becoming increasingly aware of the negative ones that surround me.
- I am able to recognise lower energy, and either raise it to a positive one, or avoid it completely.
- My judgement of all situations is becoming less and less. I can clearly see all lessons for what they are.
- I am a creator of beautiful things. I can attract beauty in all things.

- I am in control of all my reactions, I project in any negative circumstances. I am mindful of any destructive thoughts if anything unfortunate happens. I am fully aware. I can transmute this energy in to the positive energy of love.
- I am the master of my own energy field. I vibrate higher to activate my "Merkabah".
- I am an active person that enjoys having fun daily.
- I love giving joy and happiness to others.
- I share my joy with everyone I encounter. I have more than enough joy in my heart to share.
- I am hopeful always. I trust in the creator of our universe.
- I give hope to others in every way that I can.
- I am a creative creator within this realm.
- I shine my light and joy into the world daily
- I bring hope with the kind things I do, for others and myself.
- I am starting to purify my energy centres, and as I do, I become closer to the heavenly creator I serve, and one with all on earth.
- I am forever in control of my emotions and actions.
- I give and receive affection easily.

- I am in control of my feelings, and any destructive feelings. I feel and acknowledge them, and then let them pass freely without judgment.
- I am no longer under any of the illusions I was under as child, or young adult. I am awakening into my higher consciousness.
- I am full of hope for the future, for all of humanity.
- I give hope to others in times of need.
- I am on a spiritual journey of purification. I am becoming what I'm meant to be.
- I am an active, and enthusiastic person daily.
- I purify and bless the water that I put into my body.
- I cleansing my sacral chakra energy daily.
- I hydrate my body daily with water as I bless. I am truly grateful for everything.
- I am able to protect my internal emotions from lower frequencies of negativity that sometimes try to surround me.
- I am able to relate and respond in a positive manor to negative emotions. I can transmute negative emotions easily. I am a creative being, made of universe creative energies.

- I am in continual control of my words. I choose to be positive and project this to others always.
- I express my creativity in my personal ways, in spaces i am comfortable in. Although I am not afraid of anyone's judgements of me. I love, I do not hate.
- I am creative in many ways. I enjoy just being, and doing things that make me happy.
- I am connected to the universal energies of creativity that are within and around me.
- I honour my past emotional weaknesses. I am becoming emotionally stronger daily.
- I am just like water, and move with the flow of life.
- I am in constant movement and changing continually. Just alike the rivers and seasons, I am one with all.
- I share my creative ideas with others to better all.
- I am working through my karma lessons in life.
- I am a co-creator within my universal experience.
- I am working on myself spiritually and in doing so, others close will benefit from the more authentic me.
- I am always joyful and hopeful in all things that I do.

- I am surrounded with healthy relationships in my life. I am clearing any blockages in my sacral energy centre. I am a self-confident person.
- I am balanced within my sexuality, my strengths and weaknesses. I honour both in balance, as I conquer all fear, stress, and anger that came from lust. I let it all go freely.
- I spend quality time with myself in mediation. I am not afraid to be alone. I find peace and answers in the silence. I am not afraid of my darkness. I can control it with my inner light.
- I am becoming stronger emotionally, physically, and mentally in each new day.
- I see everything living in its truest nature.
- I view life with a deep creative passion.
- I am emotionally secure and my needs are fulfilled.
- My faith in love, and service to the light within others, means my desires are always granted from God.
- I don't focus too much on others perspectives of me. I am kind to myself and others. I don't need approval to be me, I am happy to just be.

- I embrace my creativity on a daily basis. I express myself freely.
- I balance my health. I drink lots of water daily to keep my body cleansed and clear from negative blockages.
- I am in control of myself and my actions always. I am responsible.
- I balance my sacral chakra centre and this supports my energy flow, and increases my intuition.
- I have an abundance of passion for my life, and the support of others.
- I radiate my warmth and light into this world. I happily share my warmth with all worthy.
- My visions are now becoming clearer.
- I generate positive emotions from any negative feelings. I am able to turn bad situations into good outcomes.
- I am becoming more in tune with my highest astral self. Each day I am grateful for the guidance I seek, and am given.
- I listen to my inner wisdom and feelings. This truly guides me safely, to where I need to be.

- I radiate passion into the souls of others. I am forever changing, flowing in motion like the tides of the ocean.
- I am now aware of habits that hold me back, and don't allow me my freedom.
- I am committed daily to developing my spiritual awareness and growth.
- I am hopeful that I will achieve whatever I want to do in any moment.
- I express my creativity in how I dance and sing.
- I am always happy and in a constant state of higher creative connection.
- I am thankful for the continual source of the universal creativity energies that flow freely to me.
- Life is school. It gives each person daily lessons until the end. I am happy to learn and let go.
- I am able to learn the lessons of life fast. I am open to receive them and transmute these energies, and then receive the blessing that awaits me after my awakenings.
- I am able to let go, and able to move forward on this journey with the confidence that I need.

- I can see the synchronicities now. I am humble I am blessed. The universe is working for the betterment of all.

Daily practice of these particular affirmations will assist you to turn around your attitude, as well as your world in no time.... These affirmations are designed to support you, with clearing negative emotional energies and thought patterns. As well as aid you in raising your awareness and natural vibration higher, so to reach optimal energy levels within. This chapter will ultimately have a positive effect on the overall control of your response and actions to your emotions in any given present, and the experiences you will have in your future life time, if you can remain mindful of the affirmations you give to the universe.

Solar Plexus Chakra Healing & Activating Affirmations

Affirmations for the Solar Plexus Chakra, will help you to open, cleanse, clear, and generate new powerful energies that will ultimately bring positive experiences for you, and your loved ones for the future. You are continually creating daily, as you think, feel, speak, and act now. When this energy centre is balanced and fully utilised, its energies can be used for the betterment of all humanity. In return this will then create the more positive and powerful co-creator within you.

- I am aligning and activating my solar plexus chakra, It is now open.
- I act courageously or compassionately, but I act according to my highest good, and the good of all.
- I have my own will power, and I get through all I need to do daily with ease.
- I am working towards divine oneness by using my gift of free will wisely, to create a better world of love, light, and peace for all.
- I am grateful for all the food available to me and that I have a healthy and balanced diet.
- I am a being of harmony, peace, and tranquillity. I radiate light and love.
- I am mentally stimulated and inspired by the actions I take towards achieving my goals daily.
- I use my personal power to better myself, and others.
- In this present, I am a positive creator always creating positive vibes, and sending them out into the world.
- I act with courage and confidence.
- I act with enthusiasm and determination.

- I will be myself always.
- I will achieve my goals successfully.
- I will never give up, as I choose goodness and love over everything else.
- My self-esteem is confident and I am healthy.
- My intellect is sharp. I am very aware of my abilities.
- My core is energised, with vitality and strength.
- I have strength and power that comes from within.
- I get things done, as I am motivated.
- I live my life with integrity.
- I think positive, and always find solutions to problems.
- I assert myself when needed.
- I set boundaries and friendships with love.
- I am authentic and natural.
- I am focused and fearless.
- I am strong. I am empowered.
- I am energized and enthusiastic.
- I know who I am. I am aligned and centred within.
- I am in control of my life in each present moment.
- I am a responsible being.
- I am successful in all ventures I set out on.
- I am ambitious and self-motivated.

- I am positively empowered.
- I am self-motivated.
- I harness my personal power, and use it to help others.
- I focus on positive outcomes.
- I have the power to manifest my dreams.
- I make my own choices.
- I use my personal power for the good of all.
- I take full responsibility for my life.
- I treat myself with respect, as I do all others.
- Success comes easily to me because I use all my energies well to align to my soul purpose.
- I use my drive and passion to better my life, as well as that of others.
- In challenging situations, I remain relaxed and positive. I choose my reaction. This is my power.
- I respect myself and others, and set necessary boundaries.
- I stand firmly, and use my personal power fully.
- I love all the powers I have, and I am willing to use them for the betterment of humanity.

- I know the energy I hold is powerful, and I understand equally its worth is greater than anything material I can manifest. I will consciously use it as a tool to assist humanity in awakening, and I will assist with providing guidance and methods of understanding, and coping with the amnesia of awakening and settling into their personal power.
- I am an endless abundance of power and energy supply.
- I use all my strengths and powers for the betterment of all.
- I am free in any given moment, to be responsible for my reaction to all situations. I choose to respond with understanding, love, and forgiveness.
- I take actions towards the directions I want to go in life.
- I express my personal power with freedom and clarity.
- I can, and will express myself in clear powerful ways.
- I am truly grateful for all the powerful and positive energies I can generate from within.
- I stand up for myself and others that are vulnerable.

- I stand up for what I feel is the right thing to do consciously.
- I am doing the best I can always.
- I am doing the best I can for myself and others always.
- I honour and respect myself. I am a powerful being.
- I honour and respect others. I used my personal power to protect humanity.
- I am grateful for the healing energy I have, and am able to use to support myself and others.
- I love and accept others as myself.
- I choose always to be courageous and strong.
- I am at one and at peace with myself and others.
- I choose only healthy relationships for my future.
- I am an original and authentic being of creation, therefore I can create.
- I am an infinite being of love and light.
- I am proud of all my actions and achievements.
- I strengthen my bond to creator and all daily, in all I do.
- I have complete control. I am confident with the outcome to come in my life.

- I am a responsible being of love and light. I am honourable and of purest of intentions.
- I am always respectful of my emotions, and the emotions of others.
- I am peaceful and tranquil. I feel energized and empowered in all I do. I gather universal energies that feed my mind, body, and soul.
- I am successful and surrounded with support.
- I realise all fears and insecurities to the divine creator and Angels, to transmute that which no longer serve me.
- I have everything I need to find my way in this world.
- I am able to make the correct choices for myself towards progression in my life. I walk my path.
- I am no longer influenced by negative people, as I am not influenced by intimidation.
- I am free to just be. I am me, and I stand firm in my new found truth that's crushing old beliefs of separation.
- I am strongly connected to the source of all power and creation.
- I shine my light of love, bright into this world.

- I never rush choices that I make for my future, because I am patient. I understand divine timing.
- I have exposed myself to my deepest fear, and fear has no longer any power over me.
- I feel no shame. I am a strong confident person.
- I am free to use my willpower to benefit others, and myself.
- I empower others with light and love energy.
- I am more than enough.
- I live with compassion, kindness, and integrity.
- I honour all the gifts, of all the energies that the Solar Plexus brings into my life.
- I stand strong and steady in my ability, and my power to help bring love into all life.
- I am able to let go of all judgements of me that have been placed on me by others. I let this go.
- I no long place judgement on others. I let this go.
- I am at peace with the world around me, and my place within it. I am a centred co-creator.
- Each new day I find things new that I love about myself and others, that travel along beside me on this journey.
- I respect myself and I respect others.

- I am caring for myself internally, as well as externally now and forever more.
- I am mighty powerful and strong, as is the energy that resides within me.
- I believe I can do anything I want to do.
- I am a co-creator of my life, and the almighty creator is my inner guide.
- I am in charge of whatever direction I choose to take, in any present moment on my life's journey.
- I am adventurous, daring, and creative.
- I stand up from myself and others when I can, and use my powers to encourage others to do the same.
- I am worthy of love, compassion, kindness, and I respect this is my birth right.
- I deserve a natural, wonderful, and magical life.
- I am who I am, and I love and accept every part of myself.
- I am powerful and pure energy source.
- I am mastering all my personal powers at present.
- I have everything I need within me.
- I deserve a prosperous, pure life. I am worthy.
- I am now content within myself, and I am healing my health through my inner abilities.

- I am spending some time meditating in the sun, which feeds my energy in many ways. I grow stronger daily, in mind, body, and soul.
- I can choose to respond with love, this is my power. I stand strong in my decisions and understanding of life.
- I am free to do whatever I like, today and tomorrow, and every day after because this is my life.
- I choose all relationships in my life based on frequency and intuition.
- I feel no shame in regretting any of my past actions, as they are of good intention, and of pure love and light for the best of all.
- I do not base my decisions on fear; I base them on respect for myself.
- My personal power now in present, is to create my future with the power of gratitude, oneness, love, joy, peace, faith, and truth.
- I am growing stronger day by day.
- The sunlight will nourish my Solar Plexus so I can radiate even more magical energy out into the world.

- Divine energy runs through every cell of my body, and I am receptive and appreciative of this energy.
- I appreciate my own power can help to heal humanity; I use my power to heal all.

Daily practice of these particular affirmations will assist you to turn around your attitude, as well as your world in no time.... These affirmations are designed to support you with clearing negative emotional energies and thought patterns, as well as aid you in raising your awareness and natural vibration higher, so to reach optimal energy levels within.

Heart Chakra Healing & Activating Affirmations

Heart chakra affirmations will assist you to open, cleanses, clear, and generates new energies. These energies will ultimately bring an overwhelming sense of peace, love, joy, and a new found gratitude for life. You will then be open to receive the abundance of unconditional love, and a bounty of universal oneness energy will be set free from within, that already resides within you.

- With every breath, I inhale positive universal energy. With every exhale, I release toxins and blockages of negative energy.
- I am aligning and activating my heart chakra. It is now open.
- My heart is always and forever in peace and bliss, when I am in my own truth.
- I am in balance with both my masculine and feminine nature. I am able to use these to my advantage. It is a great strength.
- My heart is healthy, my soul is tranquil I am connected to all.
- I am a caring and compassionate being. I am free to grow spiritually.
- I am love, I am peace, and I am of purest light.
- I am in touch with my emotions. I am able to express them freely with compassion from the heart.
- I love my life, I love myself, and all people I let into my life.
- I love being alive. I love and feel connected to the earth. I feel every caring heart here.

- I love being in nature, as my heart is naturally at its happiest here.
- I love all worthy souls close to me, deeper than any ocean.
- I will love all until the end of each time in space
- I give and receive love easily. I am the essence of love itself.
- I give compassion and acceptance, to all that deserve it.
- I receive an abundance of love from the universe.
- I receive compassion and love from all I love.
- Love and beauty surround me daily. I'm humbled and blessed.
- Love flows into my life and being.
- All of my relationships are harmonious and balanced.
- All of my being is love and light. A beautiful piece of art.
- Love is the universal language I speak.
- I forgive and love myself and others. I am open and receptive to love.
- My heart is awakened, and my heart is connected to all of life.

- My love is abundant and my heart overflows with love.
- My heart is connected to all that is, and all that ever will be.
- My heart is open to love of the purest light.
- My light is a powerful force in this world, to light and warm the way for all.
- I love and accept who I am. I love and accept others for who they are.
- I can extend love and compassion to all beings, all over the world
- I give love, not to receive love, but I receive all love with the greatest gratitude. I am very humble and blessed to have such loyal loves in my life.
- I am a being of love, for love is all that exists.
- I am a light house for those lost in the darkest oceans.
- I project my love and light to all life, as its all one and the same life source of energy.
- I just love life and appreciate all loving lights I've found within it.
- I give unconditional love to all worthy of my love.
- I live in forgiveness and love daily.

- I am cleansing and clearing my heart chakra.
- I am in love with this beautiful earth and its real beauty. I appreciate all souls that bring me love and light.
- I can see the good in all things. I see with eye of compassion and understanding.
- I reconnect all I encounter, bringing each soul back into love and light.
- I am so very happy and love to just be me. I am most happy just being in the highest vibration flow of life.
- I love to spend time with the people that I love and respect, and in return who love and respect me.
- I am a being of love and light, and I shine bright in even the darkest of nights.
- I am cleansing and clearing my heart chakra. It is now fully activated
- I bring the sunshine for all, with the love and faith I hold within my highest self, and I radiate this outward into the world.
- My heart is in perfect sync with the divine source of all creation.
- I am grateful for all the beauty and love that surrounds me.

- My heart is always and forever in light, and surrounded by the purest love.
- I radiate so much love into the world each new day.
- I deserve to receive as much love as I give to others.
- I see all with loving eyes, as well as a loving heart.
- I radiate unconditional love and light, "my song" is harmony and balance into the whole universe, and the universe radiates it back to me in the most perfect symphony.
- I feel much love within, and radiate it outwards and I do not need approval to share this with all or any.
- My heart overflows with love, and light for all life.
- I support everything of light and love with all my heart and soul.
- I cause no grief, as I only bring love and light into the hearts of souls I meet.
- I feel sadness and grief in others, these senses allow me to use my greatest healing gifts to transmute any heavy energies of the heart and mind.
- I am happy and in flow with the natural cycles and rhythm of life, and the flow within the universe.

- My love is so pure, therefore I become more peaceful each day.
- I have the highest respect for love, and the purest of all light I feel daily.
- I am so in love and grateful for the love I feel.
- I give love and forgiveness to myself and others freely.
- My heart is open and balanced. I love my life
- I am cleansing and clearing my heart chakra. It is now activated.
- My heart chakras are now cleansed and fully open.
- I am one with all and all, is now one with me.
- I am able to give everything on earth love, there is no separation.
- I am energy, and energy is everything, therefore I am everything.
- I am eternally blessed with love and light from the supreme source of all.
- My heart chakra is fully opened.
- I am generating love and light daily in all directions, and all levels of life.
- I feel great and rise higher the more love and light I give to others.

- I have an understanding and compassionate heart, that beats strong positive energy into the world for the good of all.
- I am a vessel of light and love for all.
- I am able to see the synchronicities that lead to my twin. I follow my inner flame as its one and the same spark.
- I am one with all universal energies that flow through me.
- I am comfortable to be around, and I give comforting and warm vibes. Therefore, others become comfortable in my company.
- I am welcoming love and light into my life.
- My heart energy grows stronger each new day.
- I am now appreciating everything with love and gratitude.
- I am finding new passions for all things in each new day.
- I am open to my bliss, my heaven here on earth.
- My heart is open to give plenty of love. There is more than enough love for all that crosses my path.
- I am grateful my heart is strong and healthy.

- I am one with the divine creator that created my soul, and that occupies my heart.
- I have the force of love and light within me, and I give this freely to others.
- I create all things with love through my heart.
- I embrace life, and I open my heart to love.
- I am open always to love and light, from this day forth as I accept everyone, as they accept me with love.
- I forgive everyone that's ever hurt my heart. I am stronger and wiser. I forgive myself for ever hurting anyone in my past, as I look forward to my future.
- I allow the abundance of the universe to pour into my heart freely.
- My heart radiates love and light in magnitude, as I attract only true light and love.
- I encounter love and light in all I do.
- I live my life in perfect love and light.
- My heart is grateful for all the love it has known.
- I radiate powerful unconditional love for all, as all is one.
- My heart is now open to my truest love of all.

- There is space in my heart for all that are worthy enough to occupy it.
- I am deeply grateful each day for the energy that runs through my heart.
- I am happy my heart is content and free.
- I am content and happy to be right where I am in this space.
- I do things every day to fill my heart with gratitude.
- My heart sings a song of love each new day.
- My heart lives in bliss and my body is balanced. My mind is present.
- The simple things make my heart beat in melody and love.
- I appreciate all things of beauty, these are the things that make my heart sing in tune with the universe.
- I am following the flow of my heart and its truth.
- As I release negativity from my heart it becomes lighter in love and light
- I do things each day that bring great joy to my heart.

Daily practice of these particular affirmations will assist you to turn around your attitude, as well as your world in no time.... These affirmations are designed to support and assist you in clearing negative energies and resetting thought patterns. Affirmations will aid you in raising your awareness and natural vibration higher, so to reach optimal energy levels within your heart chakra, to reset it back into a state of Inner abundance of oneness and unconditional love ....

Throat Chakra Healing & Activating Affirmations

Throat Chakra affirmations will assist and support you to open, cleanse, and clear this chakra energy centre. This will generate new energies that will ultimately bring positive experiences into your existence. When you raise your vibration from fear, you transform this inner energy into love, then you can live a life reflecting integrity in your most authentic light of self, with clarity and truth.

- I am aligning and activating my throat chakra. It is now open.
- I communicate easily, with clarity and love.
- I am creative every day. I know how to express myself freely.
- Through art, music, writing, and speaking my truth. I am expressing my spirits authenticity.
- I am aware my words fly higher than the sky, through time and space, creating pattern and form. I am a magician casting spells into the universe with my words.
- I alone am responsible for expressing myself freely. I was given a voice to express my truth.
- I feel fulfilled I am happy. I am free.
- I am loved. My needs are always met. I am truly grateful for this.
- I am not afraid to speak my mind. In doing so I use compassion and kindness.
- I respect others views and truths, as much as I value my own.

- I am open and clear when I communicate with others. I am honest in my intentions.
- I am free to express my opinions.
- I am a warrior of unconditional love, on a mission to spread light and truth.
- I have a right to speak my truth.
- I communicate my feelings with ease.
- I express myself through being able to freely speak my truth and be open with others.
- I nourish my spirit through creative expression of truth, and gratitude.
- I love to share my experiences and wisdom. I know when it is time to listen and learn truth for myself. I need to be silent within.
- I express my gratitude towards life in all ways I possibly can.
- I listen to my heart to know what my truth is.
- I speak my truth because I speak from my heart.
- I speak authentically with integrity.
- I speak my inner truth with confidence from within.
- I listen with compassion. I speak with truth.

- I listen to my inner voice in silence.
- I listen to the voice of my spirit. I can hear and feel it within me, in each present.
- I listen to others truths with an open mind and heart when they speak.
- I listen to others without judgement.
- I hear my inner voice speak loudly and clearly.
- I hear the wisdom of my intuition. I am connected and guided to speak my truth.
- I express my truth in every mindful present.
- I express my creativity with ease.
- I express gratitude towards all life, always. In all ways.
- I express myself effectively and honestly.
- I express myself with clarity and confidence.
- My voice is strong and I know, I am secure in my truth.
- My opinion is my own. I can say what I truly feel, without being rude or disrespectful.
- I can identify and express, a universal language of love and compassion.
- I am authentic. I am honest.

- I am true to myself which makes me a loyal person.
- I can create with what I speak into existence.
- I always speak from my heart, to follow it is my truth.
- In each new day, I welcome truth into my life.
- I always find new unique ways to express my inner truths.
- I acknowledge the power of my words can create what I intend.
- I am courageous and confident when expressing my truth.
- I am truth. I speak truth. I teach truth. I act and respond with truth at all times.
- I am brave and courageous. I speak my truth as I am not afraid to stand up for unity, and universal truth of oneness.
- My throat chakra is now opening and activating.
- I have the right to speak my truths.
- I communicate my feelings freely.

- I can communicate with everyone. Language has no barriers, the only frequency I hear, or express is love.
- I speak with integrity and love always, in many creative ways.
- I grow confident and secure in my truth daily.
- I nourish my body through creative expression, of love and truth.
- I am cleansing and clearing any blockages in my throat chakra.
- I can express myself creatively, through all forms of creative communication and truth.
- I live an authentic life of integrity, and of greater intentions of love and truth.
- I am in a perfect state of peace in my truth. It brings my bliss closer to me. I am a calm and creative being.
- I find my truth in silence. I am not afraid to be alone in the dark. I am the light.
- I express my truth daily, with respect and gratitude.

- I nourish my mind through creative expressions of love and truth only.
- I am an infinite being of love and light. I know my truth, as I am now confident enough to speak it.
- I am open and clear with my speech so everyone can understand me.
- I am willing to expressively share my wisdom and truth with anyone.
- I understand when it is time to listen.
- I can express myself creatively through writing and through ………whatever captures your interest.
- I am confident in all I do. I can always find new adventurous ways to express myself in.
- I am open to all universal truths that lay asleep within me. I now call them to rise and awaken for the better good of all humanity.
- When I sing songs that resonate within me, this action raises my creativity vibration higher.
- I can resolve any challenges, by expressing my inner truth.

- My throat chakra is cleared and cleansed.
- I am an expression of love and truth.
- I am grateful for very experience in my life. I express gratitude daily unconditionally, for all I graciously receive.
- I nourish my spirit through creative expressions of love and truth.
- I am open to truth. I am honest.
- I sing my hearts song. I am inspired.
- I am open to the universal truth within me.
- I am an exceptional being of understanding, and listen when I need to, and transmute negative energy into love.
- I can express and engage myself within creative communication, and express myself freely and confidently with others.
- I remain calm, collective and creative, in every situation.
- I speak up for myself and others, that are unable to speak up for themselves.
- I am an authentic and a creative being.
- I express positivity and compassion in all words I speak.

- My voice maybe soft, but it is heard when It is needed to be heard.
- I am true to my word.
- I radiate truth.
- I communicate clearly and truthfully.
- I mean what I say.
- I am following my dreams, by being true to myself.
- I use my expression creatively to bless others.
- I create my own reality in my truth.
- My highest truth is always listening, and ready to guide me towards truth and love.
- My highest self only has influence on my life's truest paths.
- My throat chakra is now open. I can channel truth.
- I am the master of my creative expressions.
- I speak love. I speak truth.
- I do what I say I am going to do.
- I do not judge others. I do not gossip, as I try to understand all.

- I express only kindness and compassion to others.
- I express my truths with clarity, and complete confidence
- I communicate my highest self through my expressions of truth. In doing so, I honour this expressive side of my being daily.
- I am a clear receiver of divine truth.
- I trust in my highest self, to guide me to truth and wisdom on my journey for the highest good of all.
- I am always truthful to myself and others.
- I believe and trust in my truth.
- I am always gentle, mindful and respectful with the words, I choose to speak.
- I am delightful and respectful to all, when in my truest nature.
- I am aligned to my highest truth now.
- I have a strong sense of myself and others truths. I have a strong, confident character, that's proud to speak the truth.
- I have as much right as the next person to speak my truth, there is no difference.

- I can express my visions clearly to others.
- I listen to understand the needs of others.
- Everyday my throat chakra energy centre is aligned, and is generating in abundance more creative expressions, of love and light into the world

Daily practice of these particular affirmations will assist you to turn around your attitude, as well as your world in no time. These affirmations are designed to support and assist you with, clearing negative energies and resetting old thought patterns. As well as aid you in raising your awareness and natural vibration higher, so to reach optimal energy levels within your life's experiences. Feelings of freedom, real clarity, integrity, wisdom and truth, which ultimately leads to an inner abundance of peace. Remain mindful or conscious of the affirmations you give to the universe in every moment, as this is the "Gift" returned to you from the universe in any "Present".

Third Eye Chakra Healing & Activating Affirmations

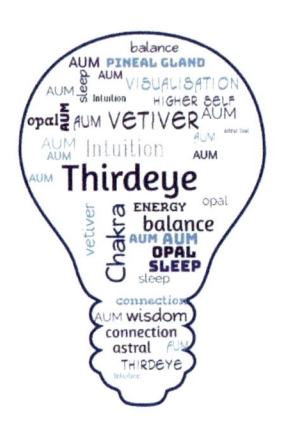

Third Eye chakra affirmations will support you to open, cleanse, clear, and generate new energies. This will ultimately bring a bounty of knowledge and wisdom, accompanied with an eternal understanding of your infinity. You will start to feel all your senses develop and strengthen, the further you continue on your spiritual journey. Your understanding of the infinite connection to creation, and all as one is within you. You are one with all in the universal ocean of collective consciousness. You are the wave.

- I trust that my third eye is opening.
- I evoke this scared transformation to open my third-eye. It is safe for me to know the truth of my infinity.
- I am aligning and activating my third eye chakra. It is now open.
- I am coming from the darkness surrounded by ignorance, into the protective light of love, knowledge and truth.
- I gather knowledge. I turn it into wisdom over time.
- I am one with my intuition. I trust my inner soul to guide me for my best purpose in life.
- My intuition is heightened. I am connected and at one with the divine source.
- I am becoming one with the light and truth, as I leave the darkness and ignorance behind.
- My pineal gland is activating. I am calm and relaxed.
- I am now opening my third eye chakra.
- I am open to truth only.

- I see through lies with my spiritual eye. I am connecting to my intuition.
- My third eye is activating and becoming stronger.
- I am one with the universal mind and I can see my future clearly.
- I master my own creation because I am my own artist. I can see clearly.
- I am deeply connected to the universal networking consciousness.
- I am one with my mind, body, and soul.
- I have total trust in my intuition.
- I see all people's present situations with clarity. I am able to see past the illusion.
- I am in tuned to all energy with my third eye. I am mastering my senses as these are all energies.
- I am starting to develop a stronger intrusion.
- I respect myself, therefore I listen very closely to my intuition.
- I am seeing everything with clarity and truth
- I am seeing everything in its truest nature, without the burden of fear.

- I am feeling Gods loving light, as it starts to flow in abundance within me.
- I can see all the wonderful opportunities life has to offer me and others.
- I trust my intuition fully. I therefore trust the truest form me.
- I see now that I am a being of spiritual collective consciousness.
- I see clearer with each new dawn, and the light within makes me grows stronger.
- I have a strong sense of my inner intuition now.
- I am connecting to my higher levels of consciousness.
- I have developed a stronger intuition now. My connection to all continually strengthens.
- My third eye is opening wider, with each meditation session.
- I can sense all signs of synchronicity clearly.
- I have an extraordinary, keen perception.
- I can see things for what they truly are.

- I am continually connected, and open to guidance from my intuition.
- I am grateful to my highest self for the connection and guidance.
- I can translate symbols in dreams clearly.
- I am continually connected to source.
- I can perceive and create the best outcome for all.
- I can sense changes in the energy that surround me.
- I can tune into my intuition, and use my energies to create my reality.
- I can easily visualise to materialise when needed, and or to help others.
- I always visualise the greatest outcome for myself and others.
- I am always using my initiative and intuition to benefit others and myself.
- I am one and at peace with my intuition and creation.
- I am aware my intuition is my best guide here. I am aware it has guided me from the

very beginning and will forever guide me to truth.
- My third eye is open and active. I can now see crystal clear.
- I am thankful my third eye is open.
- I am forever connected now to my infinity.
- I am thankful for the guidance daily, that I receive from my higher astral self.
- I am overwhelmed daily, with gratitude for the guidance and clarity my intuition serves me well.
- I am insightful and I am inspiring.
- I can see the future, because I am consciously creating mine.
- I am able to see the good and bad in everyone.
- I can see things for what they truly are.
- I am able to see the light within others and myself.
- I am no longer fooled by this lower dimensional vibration.
- I am free from illusions. I can see clearly now.

- I acknowledge my visions, and I give rise to a conscious truth that is within me.
- I am a co-creator, an artist in a dream, and in divine time I create my very own master piece.
- I am able to clearly, set intentions.
- I can see my future clearly, as I act towards create it.
- I am open to inspiration. I inspire others.
- I forgive myself for being blind, and not following my intuition for so long.
- I am connected with my Angel guides, through my intuition.
- I am guided by the ascending masters, through my intuition.
- I am able to see the patterns and synchronicities in my daily life manifest.
- I can channel deep truth and wisdom from my source conscious connection.
- I am nurturing my highest self-daily.
- I am choosing wisely what I focus spending my time on.

- I am moving toward creating my life's visions and dreams.
- I am continually expanding my awareness.
- I embrace and honour my inner knowing daily.
- I am now awakening to my greatest psychic potential.
- I am now open to receive grander visions of guidance, that will serve my souls mission.
- I am able to see what the best solutions are always.
- I can see both the lesson and blessing that are presented to me.
- I can see the best outcomes. If I focus my energy and intention on being positive, then so be it.
- I surrender to my intuition, and the divine connection.
- I know my highest astral self serves me. I know it goes before me and has my greatest purpose in hand.

- I can see, and I can feel the troubles of the world. I can transmute this energy around me.
- I am an energetic and empathetic soul, and with my personal power, I can choose to transmute the pain, and return love energy back into the world in its replacement.
- I am able to see beyond this lifetime, and see my truest nature as the veil of illusion lifts.
- I am guided daily by my intuition, visions, dreams, feelings, and signs.
- I follow my instincts, and this leads me to exactly where I need to be.
- I can see and sense, lower energy when it is close to my energy field.
- I am a powerful source of wisdom and truth
- I am able to see clearly the pieces of life's puzzle, in order to follow my fate and see the bigger picture of my destiny. I am to build.
- I am always ready to receive inner instruction from my highest teacher.

- I honour my intuition daily.
- I am able to see myself reflected in others souls, and in return see others reflect within myself.
- My spiritual vision is crystal clear.
- I am awakening to all my past life experiences.
- I am not here to impress anyone. I am content within my truth and my being.
- I now see everything crystal clear.
- I can see the whole of another's being, as clearly as I see my own.
- I choose to see the best outcome with everything and every one of my experiences.
- I can see and sense others intentions towards me clearly.
- I can see that I have the choice to change at any present moment.
- I choose to see good. I create the balance in all I do, and attract good experiences into my life.
- I am able to help others and myself, with my visions and my kind intentions.

- I see other souls' intentions clearly. I feel it in the energy they project.
- I am free to see things in whichever light, I choose to.
- I see what my truest life mission is in this carnation. I am guided, and I go with the universal flow happily.
- I am fully aligned to the greatest good of all.
- I am spiritually awakened, and now guided fully. I am open to receive this guidance.
- I am in control in each present moment, my reaction is now my own responsibility.
- I respect and trust my highest astral self fully to guide me.
- I am seeing everything differently now.
- I see through the fog and lies that's been taught to me.
- I can create anything I want to.
- I learn many new things of "truth", in each new day.
- I consume knowledge and truth like a sponge. I am now open to receive divine truth of oneness.

- I am able to astral project safely and return safely, when I want to. I am always protected.
- My intuition is on target, and I receive thankfully every answer to the questions that I seek.
- I am thankful. I am awakened to the truth that already resides within me.
- I am thankful every day for the connection I have with my highest astral self.
- I am grateful for all the spiritual guides, and the guidance that I continue to receive daily.
- I am worthy of knowing and experiencing my truest nature. I am a spiritual being having a human experience.
- The stronger my connection becomes to nature and all, then the stronger my connection bonds to the divine source of all.
- I am exactly where I need to be at any given time as I am divinely guided each present.
- I am a being of light and love.
- I am a being connected to all, for all is connected to one collective consciousness.

Daily practice of these particular affirmations will assist you to turn around your attitude, as well as your world in no time. These affirmations are designed to support and assist you, in clearing negative energies and resetting thought patterns. As well as aid you in raising your awareness and natural vibration higher, so to reach optimal energy levels within. Your knowledge and growth will infinitely blossom into wisdom, which ultimately leads to an inner abundance of clarity, unconditional love, light, peace, and knowing of your inner truth and infinity.

Crown Chakra Healing & Activating Affirmations

Crown chakra affirmations ultimately allow you to open, cleanse, clear, and generate new energies that will manifest positive experiences. As well as drawing positive energies into your life, you will create an infinite bond and connection to source creation, that will strengthen, develop and continually grow within and without, as you become one with all in time and space.

- I am aligning and activating my crown chakra.
- I am aligned to my highest self, and life's mission.
- I am fully open to receive guidance now. I am connected to source. I am now connected to the divine source of all creation.
- There is no beginning or no end to my soul's evolution. I am an infinite spirit of creation.
- I am one with all, and all is one with me.
- I am a being of love and light. I am a being of oneness.
- I am of divine oneness. I have the force of the universe behind me.
- I have the force of above, I bring it below.
- I have the force within, and bring it without.
- Universal energies surround me. I can use them to benefit all.
- My body is a temple and I will worship my highest self-daily, and the Holy Spirits light within me.
- I am one with the divine universal spirit of oneness. I am part of one collective mind.

- My consciousness is collective. I am connected to the purest light supreme.
- I am at one with my soul's path during this life's journey.
- I am part of the infinite divine source of creation. I am a co-creator.
- My mind and body are in sync with my soul's purpose.
- I am divinely inspired and guided always, in all ways.
- I am open to the energy stream of abundance, from the highest supreme of light and love.
- I am one with all, and all is one with me in every present.
- My mind and heart are in sync. I am infinitely connected to my soul's source of my creation.
- I am here to heal not harm. I am here to love not hate.
- I am here to create and not destroy.
- I am a spiritual being, having a human experience.
- I am spiritually awake. I am cleansing and clearing my crown chakra energy centre.

- I am a spiritually awakened / enlightened being.
- I honour my highest self. I honour the knowledge I have gained.
- I am wise enough to see in all creations the art of the creator.
- I am wise and gather wisdom as I go. I am always connected.
- I am always connected to the arch angels. I am fully aware they guide me when I request this guidance with gratitude.
- I am complete and feel at one with the divine energy within, and around me.
- I am going beyond limits and limitations daily.
- I honour my mind, body, and soul.
- I am strong. My faith within is Infinite.
- I am a being of the truest love and light energy within my heart.
- I am a creation of the divine architect. I am also a creator.
- I am an intricate piece within the greater mechanics of the universe.
- I am part of the universal flow. I am a being of love and light.

- I have now accepted my soul's mission. I can now see I am an infinite being of eternal light.
- I am continually working towards placing the etheric pieces to the bigger earthly picture.
- I draw truth, strength, courage and wisdom from my spiritual path.
- I am a being of purest light and love.
- I am one with nature. I am one with humanity.
- I am one with divine timing. I am one with the entire universe.
- When I am true to myself, then I am also true to others.
- I am a being of purest love. I project peace and tranquillity in to my experience.
- I live my life daily through the experiences I am guided to, by my highest astral self.
- With each new dawn, I awaken stronger in my connection to source creator.
- I am at one with all that nourishes me on a soul level.
- I am one with the whole of creation.
- Divine inspirations, spark and fuel all I create.
- Divine truth is my absolute birth right.

- I live a free life in my greatest abundance of bliss in every form, this is my birth right.
- I am a part of the divine source. I surrender my will to the Holy Spirit of all creation.
- I am living in my bliss daily. I surrender to the purest form of heavenly light and love.
- I have everything I need at this given time.
- I am free to just be. I am so very content.
- I am open to letting go of all attachments that hold me back. I know I am never apart from any energy, as it is all one.
- I am surrounded with love. I am supported in all I do.
- Others of likewise vibration, gravitate toward me. I generate higher consciousness daily.
- I serve others happily, and others serve me likewise in return.
- I know in my mind, that all is well and that I am safe.
- I am able to attract people, places and experiences, that truly nourish and serve my spirit and its highest good.

- I honour my whole, mind, body, soul, and the source creator for this experience.
- I am infinite light and eternal love.
- I am blessed, humbled and honoured, in all I do.
- I am grateful for all the knowledge and wisdom my sprit has collected through the ages.
- I am in deepest gratitude for my evolution and enlightenment.
- I am so very thankful. I am free to go beyond any limiting belief systems that try to contain or control my way of being.
- I can recognise the part of me that is a Goddess, and see the proportion of God in myself and within others.
- I cherish, nourish, and nurture my soul daily.
- I can see the wisdom within the universe.
- I am always aware, continually connected, and present.
- I am eternally grateful for every experience in my life, and all lifetimes before now.
- I know these tests and trials made me who I am today. I am grateful to understand life's truest nature.

- All experiences made me love, and for this I am truly grateful for all love energy I've experienced, and can eternally keep with me.
- I love and accept others unconditionally.
- The wisdom of the creator is within me.
- The wisdom of the universe is within me.
- I am a confident individual, living in alignment with source light and love.
- I am courageous. I do not fear anything that tries to stand in the way of divine truth.
- I am strong, free, and fearless.
- I realise that I am a co-creator in human form, here to assist in raising human conscious, awareness and vibration.
- My crown chakra energy centre is completely in sync and open.
- The universe pours an abundance of peace, love, blessings, good health and prosperity through me daily, and for this I am truly grateful.
- I am the purest form of love and light energy.
- I embrace all beings, and respect all as the same.

- I am creating love, unity, liberation, peace and equality, in all I do.
- The universe, my highest self, and all spirit guides, shower me with wisdom and miracles every day.
- I am able to transform lower energy into a higher, and more positive vibration.
- I am always open to channel divine wisdom.
- I am my own healer. I can heal others with happiness.
- I am graceful and forgiving.
- I am my own Magnus. I can manifest easily.
- I accept everything the universe offers with open arms.
- I am safe within the universe.
- I deserve only the best that life has to offer. I offer to life the best of me.
- I am always protected by my guardian angels. I need only request and be fully thankful, and they work towards gathering my requests.
- I am beautiful. I allow my light within to shine out brightly.
- I am worthy of my dreams and destiny.

- I acknowledge all my divine gifts. I am eternally grateful.
- I am an eternal being made of love and light energy.
- I am one with all of creation.
- I thrive off the highest form of light energy in my life, "LOVE" is the greatest energy of all.
- I will never again be conditioned or controlled. as I am a true spirit of love and light.
- I am free within. I am free to be without.
- I am the ultimate I can be. I am awakened / enlightened. I grow wiser along on my journey, with an infinite connection to all.
- I am a spiritual being. I am free to transmute love and light into the world.
- I am a supreme being of love and light on here on earth.
- My Crown chakra is now cleared of any blockages, and is now activated fully.

Daily practice of these particular affirmations will assist you to turn around your attitude, as well as your world in no time. These affirmations are designed to support and assist you, in clearing negative energies and resetting thought patterns. As well as aid you in raising your awareness and natural vibration higher, so to reach optimal energy levels.

Your life's experiences and feelings of the Inner abundance of love and gratitude, will transform when knowing of the infinite connection to source creator. This connection from within, will ultimately lead to an inner knowing of energy of eternal, unconditional love. This chapter will ultimately have a positive effect on the experiences you will have in your future life time. If you can remain mindful of the affirmations you give in present, is the gift returned to you

Spiritual Strengthening & Healing Affirmations

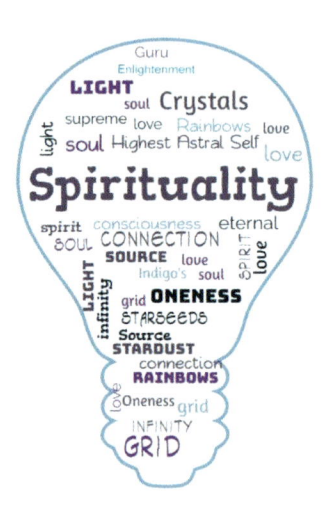

These affirmations are designed to nourish the soul's growth and expansion, with positive reminders that your highest astral self "Soul/Spirit", is always present to guide you. With clear intentions, you create a bridge to close the gap between the conscious and subconscious mind, so to secure and to strengthen your connection to source supreme collective consciousness of oneness.

- My memory is as deep as the ocean and any answers I seek
- I now understand the answers lay within the questions I seek to be answered.
- I am reaching higher levels of consciousness each day.
- I am continually connected to my higher self and original source creator.
- I am eternally grateful for all the guidance I receive from my higher self and source.
- I am aligned with the purest form of my being "who I am", I am a spiritual being, having a human experience.
- Everything I see, think, feel, speak and experience, is now tranquil and harmonised in gods flow.
- My mind, body and soul are at one with everything else in this universe.
- I am attracting others of my nature and of my kind into my experience as I vibrate higher.
- My mind, body and soul are now free to just be.
- I see no limitations. I am in harmony with life's rhythm and cycles.

- I am all about seeking my soul family only
- I am a spirit of love and light that will assist others to grow in blessings.
- I am now secure in the knowledge that I have learnt all my major life's lessons. I can now move forward in my bliss.
- I am free to continue to grow, expand and share, in all love and light with others.
- I trust my inner light to guide me. I have strong faith to be able to guide or advice others, with respect for the love and light within all.
- I am part of the all, as I am part of creation.
- I create in partnership with source creator. I am a creator in source's image.
- I celebrate and honour my higher self. It has guided me from the beginning of creation.
- I am evolving into the highest level of my collective consciousness.
- I am an open portal of divine wisdom and truth.
- I am in all things, and all things are within me.
- My connection to divine source grows stronger when I speak universal truth with light and love.

- My chakra energy centres are open and energised daily, with universal supreme love and light energy.
- I am never afraid. I am guided by a supreme and infinite being of love and light.
- I am open and always in flow, and in tune to deliver the energies the divine creator wants brings to earth.
- I am connected to every warrior of love and light to draw guidance and protection forever from these infinite sources on my request.
- I am a brilliant being of love and light. I project this with all my might into the world daily.
- The connection that I have to highest self, is as strong as the universe itself.
- I shine my love bright into the world, like the stars and moon in the night sky.
- I become higher in vibration when I give love and light to others.
- I am a master creator in this world. I know limits are illusions of fear.

- There is no end to my connection and life source within the universe. I am an infinite being of light, love, and truth.
- I am a supreme being of unconditional universal love.
- My Crown chakra is fully functional and active.
- I am able to vibrate higher above all lower frequencies, and protect my energy field in any situation.
- I am a being of electromagnetic energies and these energies are eternal, they can't be destroyed.
- I am connected to all through the unity of oneness, and the collective consciousness of the divine. I am a supreme being of light, and unconditional love
- I am love and light energy, living in my bliss.
- I am a piece of creations puzzle.
- My crown chakra is cleansed, cleared and activated.
- My energy centres are united, working in sync to excel my spiritual growth, and this flow also will assist the support and growth of others.

- I am a pure being of love and light.
- There are no bounds to my wisdom. I am connected to the universal collective consciousness, and our almighty creator's energy.
- I am a rainbow of colours within my energy centres. My enlightenment is my treasure, at the end of my inner Rainbow.
- I project love and light to the world.
- I am happily guiding others on this journey, to their inner truth and love.
- I am spirituality growing in pure love and light.
- I am drawing closer my twin energies, like a powerful magnet, the higher I vibrate.
- I am one with all the elements that surround me, and that are one within me.
- I am a natural energy force. I am an infinite soul within this universe.
- My mind is now an open portal, to expand in universal consciousness.
- My connection to source is unbreakable.
- I am now an enlightened master of my life and my infinite spirit.

- I am able to tap into source to rejuvenate my energy supply, at any present time.
- I am able to recognise whatever I need, to let go of in every situation.
- I am a supreme being of tranquillity.
- I am divinely guided in each present, in each new day.
- I am guided and grateful to the angels for the protection they give to me, on my request.
- I walk in my heaven here on earth.
- I am supreme channel to divine wisdom, and all the love within the light.
- I am one and awakened.
- I am a gifted healer, projecting light and love to anyone that is lost in the dark.
- I bring light to lost souls. I am worthy of all that I give.
- I spread my love and light, everywhere I go.
- There is no beginning or end to my love and light. I am supreme super consciousness.
- I am a highly passionate soul.
- I am an awakening/enlightened being.
- I am an infinite being of creation.

- I am my ultimate self now. I am becoming the supreme version of creations reflection.
- Every system in my body is working in balance, and in perfect harmony.
- I am liberated and I liberate others.
- I am in perfect balance with the creator.
- I am an eternal being of light and love. I am one with all. I am a being of purest supreme consciousness.
- I am as radiant as a million suns, moons, and stars.
- I am a being of clarity, purity, love, light and truth.
- I can easily transmute any negative energies that confront me.
- I am now aware my past karma has fallen, all that will arise is potential karma.
- I am aware of cause and effect after awakening and enlightening.
- I am in my most optimal state of wellbeing and perfect health.
- I am a being of creation. God and the Goddess are within me and around me.

- I am synchronised and in flow with the universe. My emotions are fully balanced within, and without.
- I am now living my optimal spiritual life's purpose.
- I am in my bliss, happily being my authentic self.
- I am without dependence. I am a confident being. I am spiritually flowing towards the union of my twin energy spark.
- I honour my highest astral self for guiding and protecting me, on each and every journey I have taken throughout time until present.
- I am eternally grateful for my future astral journeys.

Daily practice of these particular affirmations will assist you to turn around your attitude, as well as your world in no time. These affirmations are designed to support and assist you, in clearing negative energies and resetting thought patterns. As well as aid you in raising your awareness and spirits natural vibration higher, so to reach optimal energy levels within your life's coming experiences. Your knowledge and understanding of self, and your growth within spirituality will excel on the journey on which you are upon.

Virtue Bank

A

I Am -

Accepted - Achieving - Ascending - Active - Adaptable - Admired - Adorable - Affectionate - Alert - Amazing Ambitious - Articulate - Aspiring - Assertive - Angels - Ascending Masters - Awakened - Amazing Astro Project - Awesome - Accepting - Acknowledge - Abundance - Adaptable - Adjustable - Attraction Aspirations -

B

Balanced - Beautiful - Beauty - Becoming - Beloved Bless - Blessed - Blessings - Benevolent - Bold - Brave - Bright - Busy - Bliss - Blissful - Bloom Beyond Brilliant - Boss - Beliefs - Believe - Body Blockage - Bounty -

C

Calm - Capable - Charming - Cheerful - Clean - Clever - Co-operative - Collective Cosmic - Compassionate - Competent - Complimentary - Compatible - Concerned - Considerate - Courageous - Create - Creative - Conscious - Courteous - Curios - Curiosity - Creator - Crystal - Classy - Chilled - Craft - Composed - Connect - Comfortable - Confident.

D

Daring - Dazzling - Dedicated - Decisive - Delightful - Dependable - Deserve - Deserving - Determined - Devoted - Diligent - Dignified - Diplomatic - Disciplined - Distinguished - Divine - Dutiful - Dynamic - Dynasty -

E

Effective - Efficient - Ego - Elegant - Embracing - Enchanting - Encouraging - Endearing - Enduring - Energetic - Enjoyed - Enlightened Enterprising Entertaining - Enthuse Enthusiastic - Environmental Equality - Excellent Exceptional - Exciting - Expressive - Evolve - Eternal - Eternity - Emotions - Empaths

F

Faithful - Famous - Fantastic - Fascinating
Fearless - Feminine - Flexible -Fluent - Forever -
Forgiving - Forgiveness Free - Freedom -
Flavour - Funny - Favourite - Fortune - Fortunate
Favourable - Favoured - Flow - Fancy - Faith -
Faithful - Flawless - Fun - Fresh - Friendly -
Fulfilled - Frequency - Feeling - Future - Friends
Family -

G

Generous - Genius - Gentle - Genuine - Gifted
Giving - Glorious - Good - Graceful - Gracious
Grand - Great - Greatness - Grounded -Growing
Guarded - Guardian - Goddess - God - Groovy
Godliness - Gratitude - Good Vibes - Gift -
Group - Goals - Gorgeous Guru - Gaia

H

Handsome - Handy - Happy - Happiness
Harmonious - Heartfelt - Helpful - Holy -
Holiness - Honest - Honour - Honourable - Hope
Hopeful - Humorous - Humble - Hospitable -
Hero - Heaven - Heavenly - Humble - Human -
Humanity - Harmonized Health - Home -
Harmonious

I

Ideas - Illustrious - Immense - Impartial - Impeccable
Important - Impressive - Incredible - Independent -
Inspiration - Inspire Integrity - Imagination -
Investment - Intuition - Intimacy - Initiative - Intuitive
Inventive - Intelligent - Intentions - Intentional
Infinite - Incarnation — Indigos - Inventive -

J

Jolly - Joyful - Joyous - jubilant - Just be - Journey -

K

King - Kind - Kindly - Knowing - Knowledge -

L

Liberated - Love - Likeable - Lively - Loveable - Loving - Loyal- Lucky - Light - Lightworker - Luminous - Luminate Leader

M

Myself - Magical - Manifest - Miracle - Magic - Mind - Miracle - Movement - Moment - Marvellous Miraculous - Majestic - Mellow - Memorable - Merry - Mighty - Morales - Motivated - Musical - Mantra - Magnus - Magnet - Magnetic - Memories - Meditation - Mindfulness - Mission - Master -

N

Natural - Nature - Neighbour - Neighbourly - Noble - Nourish - Nourished Nurture - Nurtured Needs -

O

Oblige - One - Oneness - Outstanding - Observant - Open -

P

Patient - Peaceful - Perspective - Perceive Passionate - Pleasing - Polite - Positive - Powerful Practical - Praise - Precise - Prepared - Principles Past - Present - Peace - Privileged - Professional - Progressive - Productive Promise - Prudent Pure - Purposeful - Projection - Perfectly - Promote - Perspective - Perfect - Pretty

Q

Queen - Qualified - Quick - Quiet - Qualities -

R

Radiant - Refined - Refreshing - Reaction - Reliable - Regal - Relaxed - Resourceful - Respectable - Responsible - Rich - Royal - Reincarnation - Realistic - Reasonable - Receptive Respect - Respectful - Ready - Rainbow - Request Retrain -

S

Safe - Sanctuary - Secure - Seeing - Seeking - Selective - Self-confidence -- Sensational - Sensible - Sensitive - Sentimental - Sharing - Sub conscious - Shelter - Sound - Silence - Soulmate - Steady - Strength - Stronger - Stunning Sturdy - Stylish - Successful Super Supportive - Supreme - Sure - Survivor - Salvation - Sympathetic - Star seed - Sincere -

Skilled - Smart - Smiling - Sociable - Sophisticated - Sparkling - Special - Spectacular - Speedy - Splendid Spontaneous - Sporty - Stable - Steadfast - Success - Soul - Spirit - Spiritual - Shine - Star - Space -

T

Talented - Tolerant - Tranquil - Treasured - Triumphant - Trust - Trustworthy Truth - Truthful - Tuned - Terrific - Third Eye - Tranquil - Tranquillity - Treasure - Thought - Tone Transform - Time - Timeless - Twin Flame Tactful - Teacher - Tender - Thankful - Thoughtful - Tireless - Tolerant - Teamwork -

U

Understanding - Unforgettable - Universal Uplifted - Useful - United - Unconditional Love Unity - Universe -

V

Valiant - Valuable - vibrant - Vigorous - Virtuous - Vision - Visionary - Vibes - Visual - Vital - Victorious - Vitamins - Vitality -

W

Worthy - Wait - Wisdom - Wise - Warm - Wealthy Welcoming - Wellbeing Wholesome - Will - Willpower -- Willing - Winner - Working - Wealth - Wonderful

Y

Young - Youthful -

Z

Zestful

Daily practice of these positive affirmations will attract the progression in life you seek. Affirmations will assist you on your spiritual journey.

I would like to thank you for your support and I hope that you have enjoyed these affirmations? which were designed to assist you on your transformational spiritual journey.

I'd also encourage you to continue to practice these affirmations daily when you feel a need for change, or just need some support in general from the universe.

I wish to remind you also that, the universe only ever answers you "YES". So be sure to become mindful and think, feel, speak, and act with the greatest intentions so that the universe will reward you with its infinite answer of "YES", always in all ways.

I wish you all well on your path on this continual spiritual journey.

Eternal Love & Infinite Light.

MJ- Summers x

"As Above, So Below"

Therefore

"As Within, So Without"

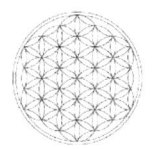

If you believe the phrase you are what you think, then life truly stems from your thoughts. Affirmations help purify our thought patterns and restructure the dynamics of our thoughts, so that we can truly begin to think nothing is impossible. Contrary to popular belief affirmations, and the power of positive thought, is not a new age technique. Affirmations can in fact be traced back hundreds of years, to the ancient East. This book is designed to help you utilize affirmations to become the best version of ourselves.

Note: These Affirmation healing meanings are for spiritual healing and support, these are not prescriptions or health care information, or for attaining approval of "Self". When one works towards bestowing "Good Will," putting these actions, feelings, intentions, thoughts and wishes out into the world towards others, and self. Thus, encourages excels one's enlightenment and one's interactions and overall service to humanity.

I would like to give much thanks to ALL reading, for your continued support. If you enjoyed this book, I would like to invite you!!, to continue reading my collection of books.

I would like to wish you all the very best, along with my love & light for the journey ahead and remember that! Nothing can dim the "Divine, Eternal Light & Love" that shines from deep within you. These gemstones are tools, to complement and enhance one's energies ONLY, the real change comes from within, Ase.

Additional Universal You Books Available
Affirmations:

- Life, Love & Light Affirmations.

Michelle Summers
Universal You Life, Love & Light Affirmations

Additional Universal You Books

- Crystals & Precious Gemstones – For the Root Chakra Energy Centre.

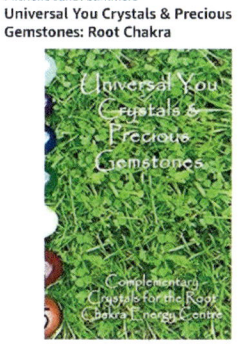

Michelle Janet Summers
Universal You Crystals & Precious Gemstones: Root Chakra

- Crystals & Precious Gemstones – For the Sacral Chakra Energy Centre.

Michelle Summers
Universal You Crystals & Precious Gemstones: Sacral Chakra

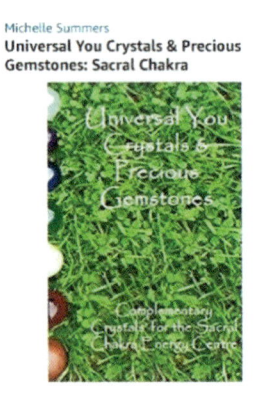

- Crystals & Precious Gemstones – For the Solar Plexus Energy Centre.

Michelle summers
Universal You Crystals & Precious Gemstones: Solar Plexus

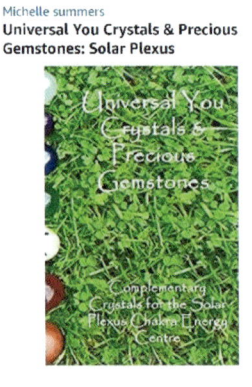

- Crystals & Precious Gemstones – For the Heart Chakra Energy Centre.

    Michelle Janet Summers
    Universal You Crystals & Precious Gemstones: Heart Chakra

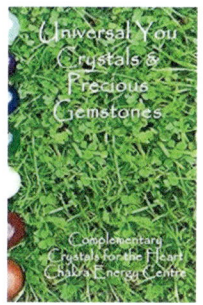

- Crystals & Precious Gemstones – For the Throat Chakra Energy Centre.

    Michelle Summers
    Universal You Crystals & Precious Gemstones: Throat Chakra

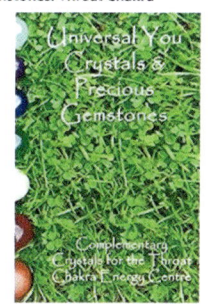

- Crystals & Precious Gemstones – For the Third Eye Chakra Energy Centre.

Michelle Janet Summersgill
Universal You Crystals & Precious Gemstones: Third - Eye Chakra

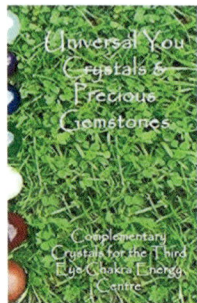

- Crystals & Precious Gemstones – For the Crown Chakra Energy Centre.

Michelle Janet summers
Universal You Crystals & Precious Gemstones: Crown Chakra

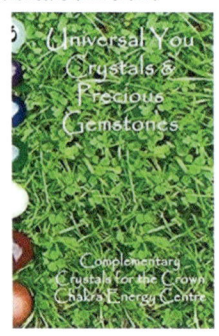

Thank you for reading.... Blessings
Love & Light as you go!!
from myself, Mj-Summers.

oxoxox

Michelle J Summers   @Universal You.

Dearest Josie x

Thankyou for your light, thankyou for your presence of Love here.

May the supreme source of All, awaken within you, hold you, heal you & lead you home...

May you eternally shine & bathe other seeds in your divine lovelight. May you be kept safest while you walk upon your divine path on Gaia. May you be blessed with a full & loving life, May you be gifted to give such pure love in all you do, say, seek & touch - Eternal Love & light.